# BLESSED NAMES

## WHY WAS HE NAMED ALI (A)?

### WRITTEN BY:
### KISA KIDS PUBLICATIONS

Please recite a Fātiḥah for the marḥūmīn
of the Rangwala family, the sponsors of this book.

All proceeds from the sale of this book
will be used to produce more educational resources.

## Dedication

This book is dedicated to the beloved Imām of our time (AJ). May Allāh (swt) hasten his reappearance and help us to become his true companions.

## Acknowledgements

*Prophet Muḥammad (s): The pen of a writer is mightier than the blood of a martyr.*

True reward lies with Allāh, but we would like to sincerely thank Shaykh Salim Yusufali and Sisters Sabika Mithani, Liliana Villalvazo, Zahra Sabur, Kisae Nazar, Sarah Assaf, Nadia Dossani, Fatima Hussain, Naseem Rangwala, and Zehra Abbas. We would especially like to thank Nainava Publications for their contributions. May Allāh bless them in this world and the next.

## Preface

*Prophet Muḥammad (s): Nurture and raise your children in the best way. Raise them with the love of the Prophet and the Ahl al-Bayt (a).*

Literature is an influential form of media that often shapes the thoughts and views of an entire generation. Therefore, in order to establish an Islamic foundation for the future generations, there is a dire need for compelling Islamic literature. Over the past several years, this need has become increasingly prevalent throughout Islamic centers and schools everywhere. Due to the growing dissonance between parents, children, society, and the teachings of Islam and the Ahl al-Bayt (a), this need has become even more pressing. Al-Kisa Foundation, along with its subsidiary Kisa Kids Publications, was conceived in an effort to help bridge this gap with the guidance of ʿulamah and the help of educators. We would like to make this a communal effort and platform. Therefore, we sincerely welcome constructive feedback and help in any capacity.

The goal of the *Blessed Names* series is to help children form a lasting bond with the 14 Māʼṣūmīn by learning about and connecting with their names. We hope that you and your children enjoy these books and use them as a means to achieve this goal, inshā'Allāh. We pray to Allāh to give us the strength and *tawfīq* to perform our duties and responsibilities.

With Duʾās,
Nabi R. Mir (Abidi)

Kisa Kids Publications
4415 Fortran Court
San Jose, CA 95134
(260) KISA-KID [547-2543]

# An Introduction to the Blessed Names

Our names are a very special part of us. Many times, they shape our personalities and even explain who we are or the person we would like to become. In this series, you will explore the names and titles of our beloved 14 Ma'soomeen. Did you know that their names and titles were not just ordinary names? They were special because they were given to them by Allah!

Allah has given seven special heavenly names to our Ma'soomeen: Muhammad, Ali, Fatimah, Hasan, Husain, Ja'far, and Musa. Behind each of these names is a heavenly power!

In addition to their names, each of the Ma'soomeen also had special titles by which they became famous. Their titles were often given to them because of the circumstances of their time, but these titles and characteristics were common amongst all the Ma'soomeen. For example, Imam al-Baqir (a) was known for spreading knowledge because he was able to create many new universities and branches of knowledge during his time. However, if the other Ma'soomeen had the same opportunity, they, too, would have spread knowledge and created universities in their teaching circles. In these stories, you will discover some of the reasons why the Ma'soomeen received their specific names or titles.

Many of us share our names with these beloved Ma'soomeen or know people who do. Let's learn about these blessed names and titles so we can strive to be like our blessed Ma'soomeen!

I think Ali means...

_____

It was a peaceful Friday morning in the month of Rajab as the sun rose up, gleaming upon the palm trees. All of a sudden, the silence was broken by the cries of a woman as she struggled toward the Holy Ka'bah. It was Fatimah bint Asad! She was crying out in pain as her unborn child was ready to enter the world.

As she reached the Ka'bah, she leaned against its walls and whispered, "O Allah, I ask you to please help me for the sake of Prophet Ibrahim (a), who built this Ka'bah. Please make the birth of this child easy for me."

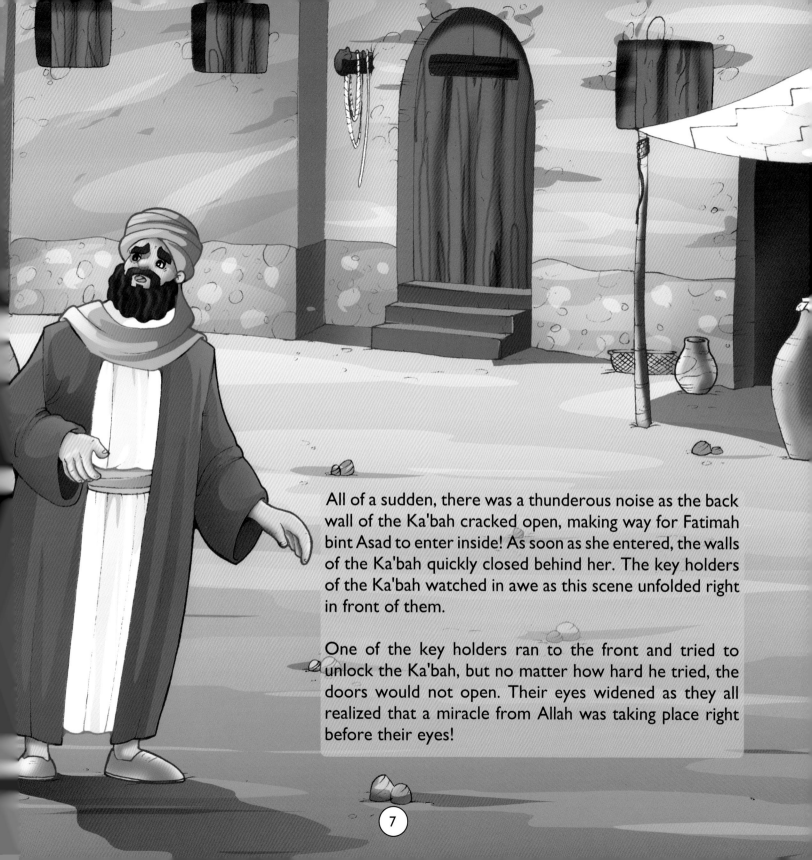

All of a sudden, there was a thunderous noise as the back wall of the Ka'bah cracked open, making way for Fatimah bint Asad to enter inside! As soon as she entered, the walls of the Ka'bah quickly closed behind her. The key holders of the Ka'bah watched in awe as this scene unfolded right in front of them.

One of the key holders ran to the front and tried to unlock the Ka'bah, but no matter how hard he tried, the doors would not open. Their eyes widened as they all realized that a miracle from Allah was taking place right before their eyes!

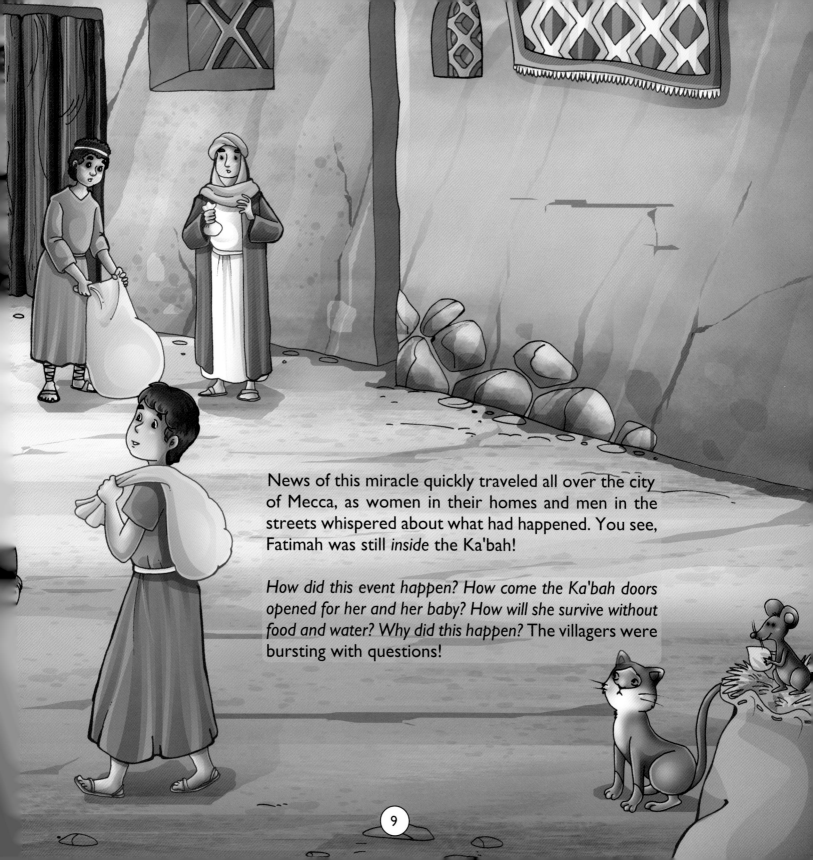

News of this miracle quickly traveled all over the city of Mecca, as women in their homes and men in the streets whispered about what had happened. You see, Fatimah was still *inside* the Ka'bah!

*How did this event happen? How come the Ka'bah doors opened for her and her baby? How will she survive without food and water? Why did this happen?* The villagers were bursting with questions!

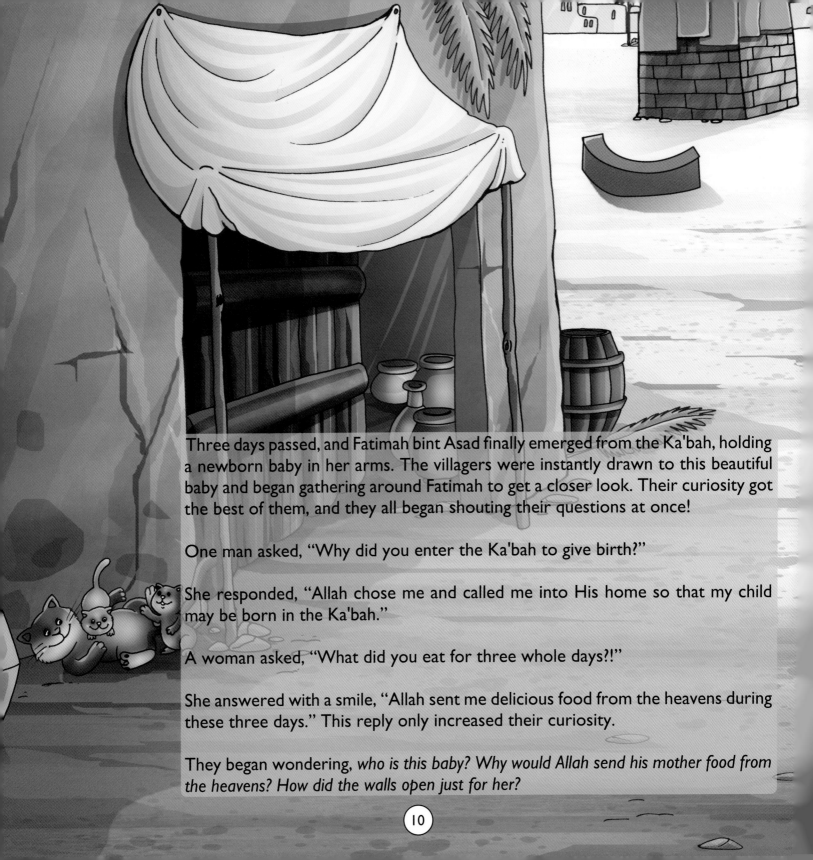

Three days passed, and Fatimah bint Asad finally emerged from the Ka'bah, holding a newborn baby in her arms. The villagers were instantly drawn to this beautiful baby and began gathering around Fatimah to get a closer look. Their curiosity got the best of them, and they all began shouting their questions at once!

One man asked, "Why did you enter the Ka'bah to give birth?"

She responded, "Allah chose me and called me into His home so that my child may be born in the Ka'bah."

A woman asked, "What did you eat for three whole days?!"

She answered with a smile, "Allah sent me delicious food from the heavens during these three days." This reply only increased their curiosity.

They began wondering, *who is this baby? Why would Allah send his mother food from the heavens? How did the walls open just for her?*

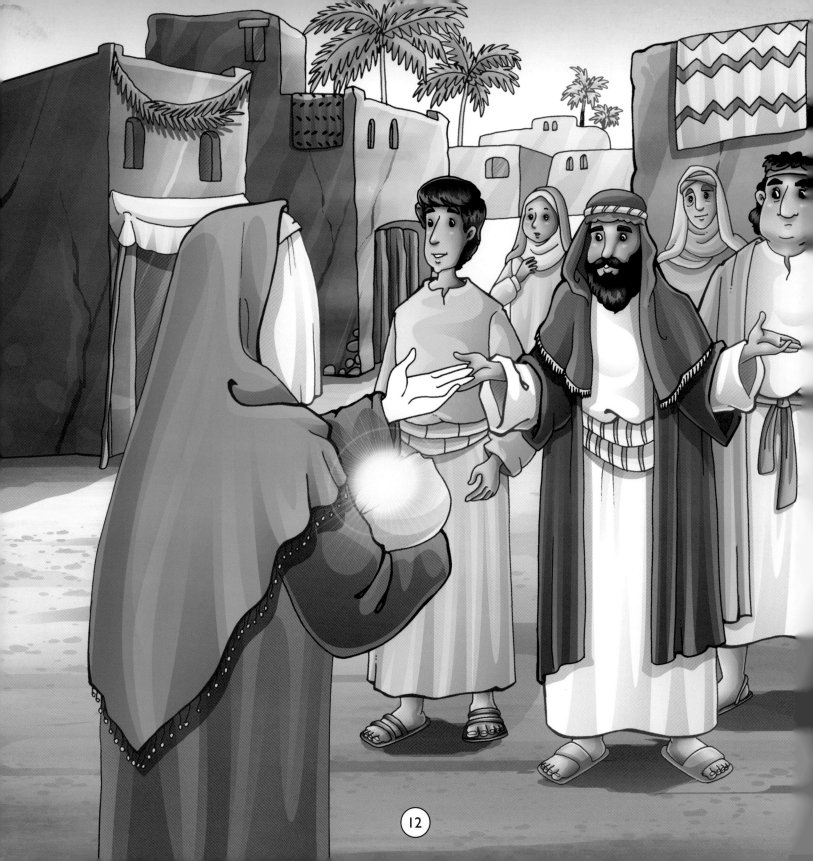

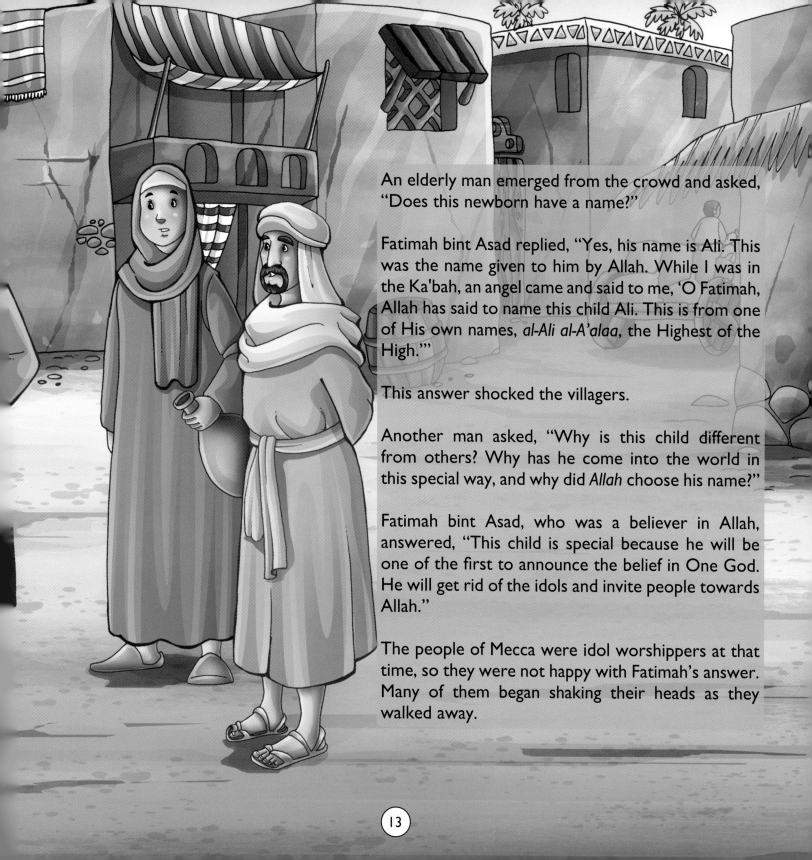

An elderly man emerged from the crowd and asked, "Does this newborn have a name?"

Fatimah bint Asad replied, "Yes, his name is Ali. This was the name given to him by Allah. While I was in the Ka'bah, an angel came and said to me, 'O Fatimah, Allah has said to name this child Ali. This is from one of His own names, *al-Ali al-A'alaa*, the Highest of the High.'"

This answer shocked the villagers.

Another man asked, "Why is this child different from others? Why has he come into the world in this special way, and why did *Allah* choose his name?"

Fatimah bint Asad, who was a believer in Allah, answered, "This child is special because he will be one of the first to announce the belief in One God. He will get rid of the idols and invite people towards Allah."

The people of Mecca were idol worshippers at that time, so they were not happy with Fatimah's answer. Many of them began shaking their heads as they walked away.

When Fatimah arrived home, she was greeted happily by her husband, Abu Talib, who joyfully took the baby boy into his arms.

Abu Talib thanked Allah and began asking his wife about what had happened. After listening to his wife's story, he felt honored to have such a special child. As the day turned into night, Abu Talib and his wife, Fatimah, journeyed to the Desert of Abtah to thank and pray to Allah for their beautiful baby.

They walked and walked until they reached a place where no one could see them. Abu Talib held his son in his arms and cried out, "O Allah, the Greatest, You created the darkness of the night and brightness of the moon. Tell me, what is the wisdom behind this child's name?"

Suddenly, the clouds gathered and the wind started blowing ferociously. Abu Talib tightly clutched his son as they were suddenly surrounded by a great storm. Then, just as it came out of nowhere, the storm stopped abruptly and Abu Talib headed back home with his wife and son, puzzled by what had just happened.

When they reached home, Abu Talib found Baby Ali (a) clutching a divine note in his tiny hand that read, "We have blessed you with a pure and great child. His name is 'Ali,' which means 'the high.' This name has been chosen for him because he has a high position in the eyes of Allah." Tears filled Abu Talib's eyes as he fell into sujood and thanked Allah for this great blessing.

As the sun rose the following morning and people gathered around the Ka'bah, they couldn't help but notice how the crack in the Ka'bah almost seemed to be smiling.

O Allah, send your peace and blessings upon Imam Ali (a), 'the high,' who showed the highest levels of *taqwa** and akhlaq!

Kashf ul-Ghummah fi Maʿrifah al-Aʾimmah, Vol. 1, P. 79-80

*Taqwa: Being God-conscious and guarding oneself against that which Allah has forbidden.